Become As A Child

Centering in the Light of Grace

Wanda Morgan

authorHOUSE®

AuthorHouse™
1663 Liberty Drive
Bloomington, IN 47403
www.authorhouse.com
Phone: 1-800-839-8640

First published by AuthorHouse 3/11/2010

ISBN: 978-1-4490-8662-6 (sc)
ISBN: 978-1-4490-8663-3 (e)

Library of Congress Control Number: 2010903193

Printed in the United States of America
Bloomington, Indiana

This book is printed on acid-free paper.

Other books by this author:

The Nature of Centered Emotion
Pictographics

*"Except you be converted
and become as little children
you shall not enter into
the kingdom of Heaven".*

Matthew 10.19

Dedication

This book is dedicated to the memory of my daughter
Sherry who spent the last years of
her life searching for peace and the meaning of life.
After her death her final message came
to me in a dream, "Your confirmation lies within".

Contents

A Personal Introduction

My two week experience of heaven on earth began as every other day as I woke to the drudgery of twelve years of a marriage gone bad and the demands of a housewife of the early nineteen seventies. Anger at the world in general masked my depression and got me through another joyless day.

Late that evening, in desperation, I picked up a book promising a better way of life. As I read, something magic happened in my mind and I looked up from the printed page in wonder and saw that my surroundings were bathed in unexplainable glory. I do not remember the name of the book, or the passage I read, for the lighting came from somewhere deep inside me as a veil was removed from my eyes releasing me from a darkness of vision. In an instant I went from feelings of despair to joyful emotional release.

For two weeks following this incident, I was privileged to experience a wonderland of spiritual vision blended in perfect harmony with the material world. I exalted in my own "being" and in the beauty of all things physical. My eyes were opened to the moment, with no sense of past or future.

I saw the design of a leaf reflected in the palm of my own hand. The whispering wind stirring the branches of trees simultaneously stirred my senses and I was one with them. I shared in consciousness with the spiritual essence and beauty of all material things.

For fourteen days I knew what it was like to view without judgment those things I would have considered being evil. I knew how it felt to be free of fear and worry for each moment itself was completion.

On the fifteenth morning I woke to a flat, cold, gray appearing world. The light of my insight had dimmed and the magical gift of clear sight had been removed from my vision. Even as I felt a great loss I determined to consciously find my way back to the wonder of clear vision that had been mysteriously revealed to me.

A few months later, I suffered a back injury that left me severely handicapped for the most part of a year. My search for healing reached an intense pitch as I prayed night and day with great faith that I would be healed.

I had never been a religious person but in that year I felt compelled to read the bible and I came to know the love of Jesus Christ. St John the Baptist became my mentor as I read of the healing light to come. As I experienced the compassionate love God has for us I knew God and his son are One even as we all are one.

My focus moved from my pain and disability as I began sensing symbolic mental light images of geometric design which I now know are called mandalas. (I did not know at the time these images even had a name). I dreamed of moving squares becoming diamonds and turning into perfect circles of white light. The squares were symbolic of materialism, the diamonds of relationships and the circles of completion. I spent many hours translating these dream images to drawings.

While the symbolic meaning of some of these symbols were revealed to me in dreams, I became aware that I was also sensing the emotions of those around me. As I did this the emotional template of "Oneness" we share became foremost as I "tuned" in to the emotions of willing family and friends. I began to sense deeply the duality and self disapproval dominating human emotion.

Over the next few years, I completed a book I called "The Nature of Centered Emotion", with the information I had received, however I was never satisfied that I had reached my goal. I presented that book as homespun psychology and omitted the spirituality for those days were different than now and so was I, for I thought my mystical experience would not be understood.

Many years passed during which I continued to observe the emotional reactions of myself as well as others. Several years ago I felt urged to re-write the message of the Mandalas, this time complete with the spiritual origin.

This book is the culmination of a twenty - five year search for a return to the state of grace that was revealed to me. The final message as related in this book, is that enlightenment is not some elusive esoteric search without end but a return to my beginnings. In order to do that, I needed to understand how, I myself, was blocking my awareness of the centered state of grace that was already mine.

In a wedding of the material and the spiritual sixteen mandalas encompass a structure containing both the conditioned emotional responses of materialism and the light giving spiritual support that lives in and through our center of consciousness. In a revelation of self awareness painful errors in ego identification are compassionately revealed and replaced by a quintessential spiritual healing.

Even though, I personally, felt drawn to read the new testament of the KJV Bible, and have included some of the scriptures in this book (as well as other notable quotes) I feel that enlightenment comes in many forms and beliefs. I believe in the existence a Harmonic Universal consciousness that governs us all and to all the healing gifts of spirituality are given).

Preface

Mandala

A picture speaks a thousand words

As the Mantra is to the audio so the Mandala
Is the visual guide to spiritual Centering. Mandalas
Are as the hieroglyphics of the angels, revealed
To earthly consciousness, giving form to intuitive
knowledge and enlightenment.

Mandala of Centered Vision

We all sit around and suppose
While the secret in the Center
Quietly knows.

William Blake

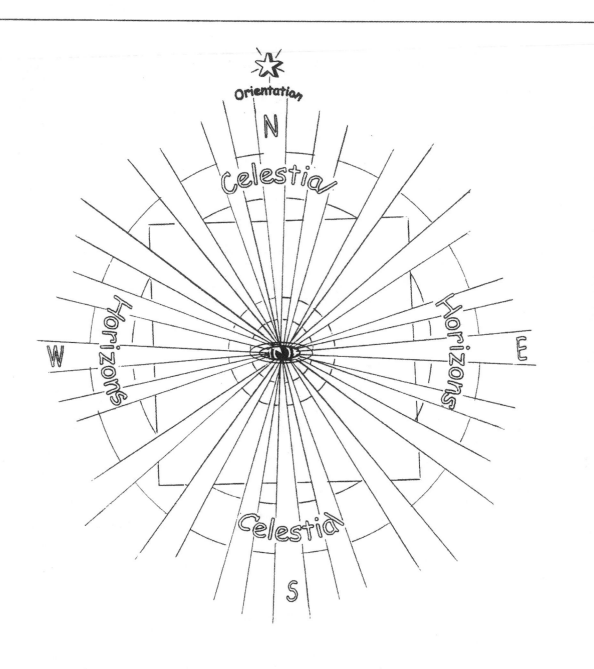

The light of the body is the eye
Therefore, if thine eye be single
Thy whole body shall be full of light

Matthew 6.22 KJV

Mandala of Centered Vision

As the north star directly above you orients you to a celestial environment, the lighting of the center of the mandala is symbolic of your innate Centered vision.

The stillness that is the first of you.

Beneath the din and clamor of your thoughts while focusing on the material world is a treasury of peace and quiet knowing. The light of heaven is the lighting of your earthly consciousness. As such you were born centered in your physical and mental being. This lighting is of the life force living out a mission through your physical existence. Subservient to your material focus is your *spiritual guide: Your first state of consciousness.* This compassionate center of your self is a magical one for as it lives with you and through you it also has awareness of the special plan and reason for your earthly journey. As this evolutionary being you are an earthly/celestial expression of life.

Your ability to see clearly from the spiritual lighting of your center remains subservient to your outward focus on life. Free will has been given to you so that you may learn the ways of the world for yourself. No other can reveal the meaning and purpose of life for you. As an individual you have been sent to earth to accomplish what only you can do as you contribute your chosen energies to earthly experience. You have been endowed with the powers of the God consciousness. However you may conceive of your personal God, these highest powers find a home in your mind.

In the terrestrial/celestial consciousness all things exist, from the basest to the sublime. You have been given the freedom of choice and your choices reflect your personal evolution through an *in the body experience.* As creatures of free will, we walk, talk, and sleep without really knowing how or why this happens. As an intelligent form of life we begin to question the reason for our existence. This question is met with the mentality that falls under the laws of logic and as no proof appears to exist the answer remains elusive. We must look to the laws of the universe where questions are answers and the restrictive mentality of the present stage of evolution falls away. The knowledge we crave is for deliverance from the archaic dominate negative emotional experience of life as it now exists on earth.

Each person on earth is a unique expression of life in evolutionary form. For within each person a guiding angel awaits the waking of its earthly partner. In your personal search for evolvement you are being prompted to join with this spiritually oriented self you subconsciously know dwells within you. You may have referred to this concept of your evolved self as your higher self. Begin to think of your evolved self as your Centered self, grounded in knowledge of all that you are, for there is no one or no thing higher or lower than yourself.

Many of the confusions that led you to search for answers are illusions conceived in darkness masquerading as truth. It is possible to live an entire life mesmerized by this illusionary dream. You must be prepared to delve into that part of your consciousness that you would prefer not to disturb, but to disturb in this instance is to release negative energies you have sustained for a lifetime.

Become as a Child

A smile has many meanings
As also does a tear,
The halo may be masquerade,
To alleviate a fear.

☺☺☹☺☺☹☺☺☹☺☺☹

Become as a Child

As a very young child you carried within your consciousness the glory of living matter. Your adult struggle for attainment of such consciousness is not as much a going forward as it is a returning to your beginnings.

Emotionally descriptive words, such as innocence and guilt, are illustrated by child like facial renditions familiar to you as a child. As you shed the veneer of the worldly wise you reawaken to dormant knowledge, and see again, through the eyes of a child.

Caricature like drawings of emotionally revealing faces tell simple truths in the most effective way, in pictures easily understood. Representing positive and negative emotional experience's these childlike faces become symbols eliciting personal interpretation. The use of these universally understood symbols make possible a simple presentation of complex conflicting emotions (eliminating the need for endless descriptive passages) while enhancing the innocence of spiritual awakening.

Part One

Birth of a Consciousness

As the seed of an idea, held in universal mind, living matter came to be. As is the way of earthly things, the seed or origin, disappeared from view and the species representing life appeared to stand alone.

Mandala One

Star of Spiritual Consciousness

Positive Higher Mode of Innocence

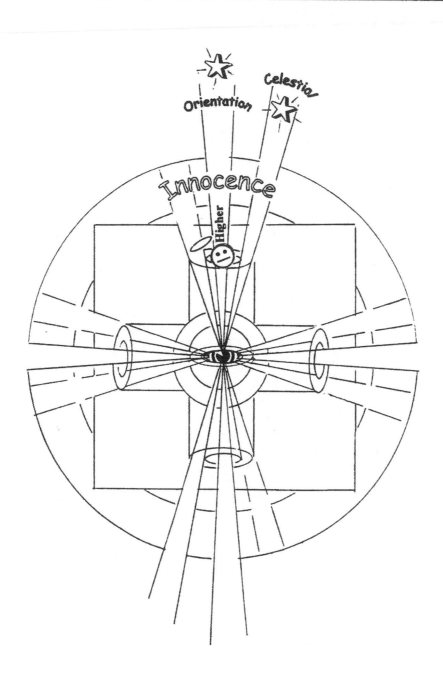

At birth your spirituality was evident to all. The light of heaven reflected in the eyes of your caretakers as they remembered, in a feeling way, their home of long ago.

Star of Spiritual Consciousness

Positive Higher Mode of Innocence

Through your centered vision you see a small face above you, floating in modules of ego and worldly experience. A vision of an angel reflects a memory of who you were. Each thing you saw you saw through the eye of an angel. This physical world was one of beauty for you had yet to learn the worldly art of comparison. From this heavenly vision you saw with no sense of judgment or evaluation. There was simply a marvelous viewing of things as they existed.

An angel came down and met with the earth
As spirit wed matter, this was your birth.
You knew not of this you thought you were all,
Yet wept, in your heart, because of your fall.

Mandala Two

Star of Terrestrial Consciousness

A sense of Center separation was inevitable, as a preordained fall from grace, at birth, influenced your emotional consciousness.

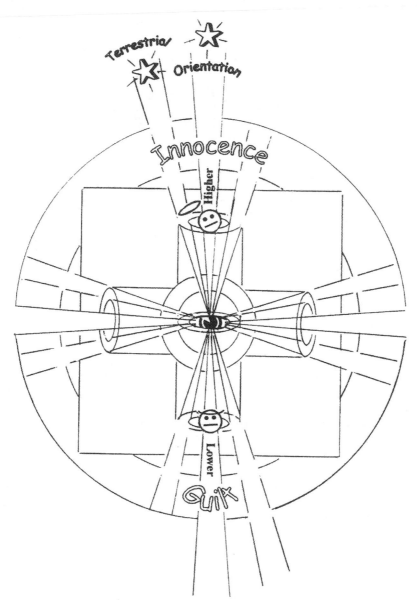

Star of Primal Consciousness

As the dual forces of the physical world claimed you for its own, a fallen angel appeared, the antithesis of the angel above. The higher angel you sensed yourself to be fought for supremacy over this lower self image and your spiritual lighting dimmed as you surrendered to the attraction of ego awareness.

Fall From Grace

Positive Higher Mode of Innocence
Vs.
Negative Lower Mode of Guilt

You do not remember that before you were born you agreed to enter conditions that would provide fertile ground to further your spiritual growth. As you came to focus more fully on the material world, the grace and peace known to a prior consciousness dimmed and faded from memory.

You came to believe, in time, that you were a product of and a possession of your caretakers... and they believed this also, as a veil was drawn over the earth, concealing true heritage from human vision. Your childhood experiences were sketched, shaded and made to appear real against a background created by angels unaware of their mission on earth. To err is human and some of the errors made by humans seem unforgivable and you may hold these errors against those people who were your caretakers.

Your caretakers may have been your biological parents, or they may have been others who came to share this time on earth and learn through earthly experience with you. Whether your caretakers were biological or surrogate parents, the roles they assumed were the same, for life is given of heaven and no other and pure non-judgmental love is the heavenly way and no other for the ways of materialism demand discrimination for survival. To discriminate is to tell the difference between, and therefore a judgmental consciousness of a sort is inevitable to life on earth.

Become as a Child

Although your emotional development was highly influenced by exterior circumstances your childhood emotions were by no means merely a result of those influences. You were born with a predisposition of conscience, creativity, and will, according to the evolutionary plan. To say you are a unique manifestation of life's energies is an inadequate metaphor for the complexities of the evolutionary chain are infinitesimal.

You entered life on earth with preconceived instinctive awareness of who you are. While you may view your "baby" self as a lump of unformed clay sculpted into form by the untrained hands of your caretakers, this is not true. The adult you came to be is also a consequence of your innate evolutionary sensitivities different from all others.

The common fall from grace

The fall from grace that was your experience at birth, was also the experience of your caretakers. In this fall all must experience the loss of innocence and the resulting loss of self worth. Emotional injuries, real or imagined, inflicted upon you by your caretakers went unnoticed by them as they too floundered in a sea of resentment and self -deprecation.

In viewing your caretakers as co-seekers on the same evolutionary journey as yourself you will stop looking at them as responsible for your adult peace of mind or for your personal validation.

Mandala Three

Self Esteem

Negative Inner Mode vs. Outer Positive Mode

Hostility sensed from the outer world mirrored negative self-reflections as you immersed your soul in your earthly environment. As a chameleon your center of "self-consciousness" submitted to the dualistic nature of life on earth. Your self-esteem was as changeable as the wind, strong and gusty one moment and silent and still as a whisper the next, ever dependant upon acceptance or rejection from others.

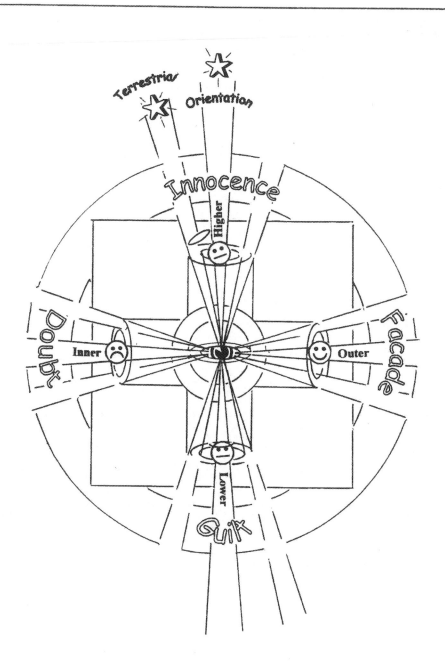

Two more, divided against each other, came into being. Your smile camouflaged your despair as the greatest treasures on earth, approval and acceptance were denied you.

Self Esteem

Overt Confident Façade
Vs.
Covert Insecurity

You learned that how you felt inside was unacceptable in many ways and you pretended to be otherwise through a façade you presented to the world. Your Inner Mode became guarded while your Outer Mode bore the burden of pretense.

You learned to conceal from others those things about yourself you deemed unacceptable and sorrow entered your soul as you carried a burden of unworthiness it seemed no one else had to bear. There was a darkness inside that must not be revealed. You smiled a smile that failed to reach your eyes. Self judgement blurred your vision and you often saw reality through a veil of tears.

In the early years of childhood you retained a sense of spirituality that acted as a buffer between your sense of self and the exterior world. As your world expanded to include the harshly discriminatory ways of childhood peers, fears of being "left out" or "not chosen" were common emotional experiences as you interacted with others in search of your own identity.

Negative input fell on fertile ground and was accepted as confirmation of what you feared in your heart to be true. As a child yearning for the consummate experience of profound and complete acceptance you were left with a feeling of deficiency; a wanting deep inside for a confirmation of self worth that never came.

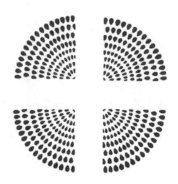

Mandala Four

Primal Centering

"I Love me" - "I Love me not".

The human animal is a being whose inner most nature is a tension of the opposites. Science calls this being energy, for energy is like a living balance between the opposites.

Karl Jung - On the Nature of the Psyche

Bollinger series

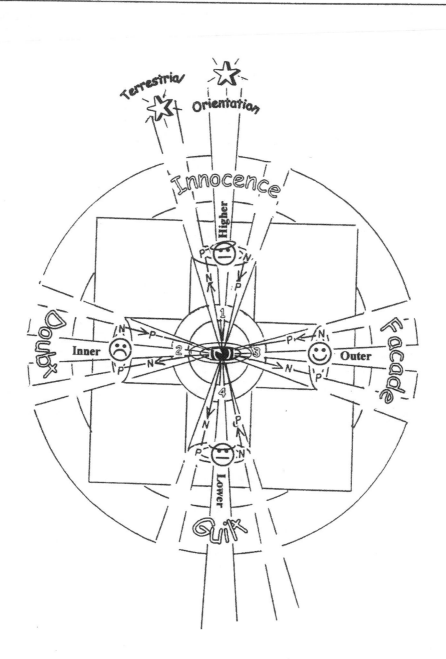

Circuitry of Emotional Duality

Childhood impressions buried deep in your subconscious mind perpetuate these opposing states of being in a constant struggle for emotional balance.

Primal Centering

Through symbolic mental channels, simulating positive and negative leads, light rays issuing from the center of the mandala form a circuitry and basic flow pattern encompassing your Primal modes culminating in your central emotional focus of any given moment.

A daisy chain of emotional current, "I love me", "I love me not" sets the cadence, the rise and fall of your Primal Center of subliminal emotional tension where ghosts of childhood self images and emotions still live. Though memories have dimmed and some are gone from conscious recall, they have left their mark on you. They appear again and again in the composite of your adult personality as an emotional collage constructed by a child unaware.

Your childhood experience, both good and bad, were necessary to the building of the fundamental foundation of your adult personality. To blame events and people contributing to your negative emotional experiences is an exercise in futility and serves to avoid turning to the insights that cause an emotional healing.

As a child you saw through the eyes of a child and the emotional heritage of this child remains with you today. While living from this heritage, you are not experiencing each day with clear vision. You came to know yourself as a child, but you have yet to learn who you are as an adult. It is true, you have learned many things you did not know as a child, but you have also learned to conceal unacceptable feelings from yourself as you came to believe you have outgrown childish ways. It is not necessary to bring to conscious awareness the things that disturbed you as a child, for you need only observe these emotional ghosts acting out in your personality today.

* * * *

As DNA contains the blueprint of individual life forms, so the mental/emotional circuits linking your Primary Modes of emotion contain a blueprint of your childhood emotional experiences. The personal experiences of your Higher/Lower - Inner/Outer Modes are intricately interwoven in your subconscious emotional processes.

Every emotion flowing through your being is rooted in this four-fold mental schematic, organizing and comparing, resulting in your personally Centered emotional experience of the moment. In a cyclic manner your first learned emotional responses echo and re-echo, resounding throughout your mental/ biological/emotional system, influencing the reality of who you feel your self to be.

* * * *

Part Two

Ghosts
Of
Childhood Past

The tears and defenses of an unjustly accused child.

Mandalas
Five & Six

Ego Defenses

(Self Pity & Self Justification)

As self worth was dependent upon outer circumstances for confirmation, the inclination to mentally alter those circumstances to reflect yourself in the best light beckoned as the Pied Piper leading you away from the truth of who you were. What was real and what was imagined co-mingled, creating a mirage of your personal emotional reality. Forced smiles, tears and anger often became your defenses against the harshness of the world.

Emotional self preservation came through as your transgressions dissolved in thoughts of self pity and self justification. The tendency to feel sorry for yourself and to justify your actions, were internalized face savers as a basic sense of self worth was mandatory for survival.

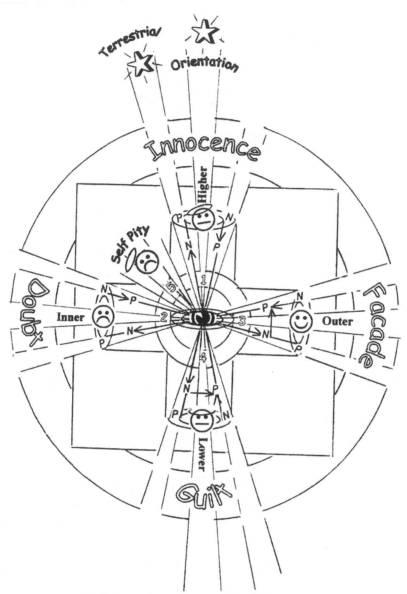

Lighting the ghost of self pity

In search of self worth, self pity rose from feelings of innocence and insecurity. Instead of bringing the comfort you hoped for, the ghost of self pity claimed and depleted your energies, defining you as a loser in your own eyes.

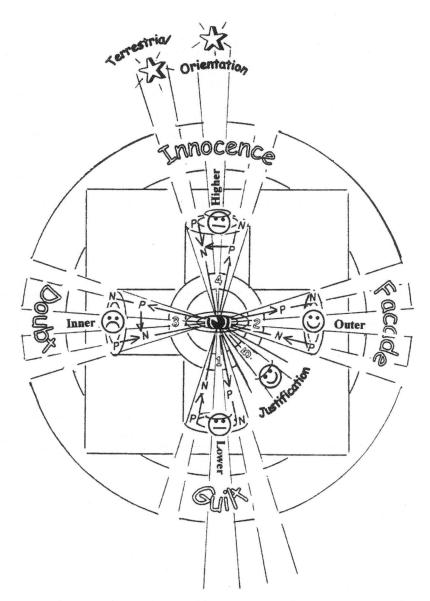

Lighting the ghost of self justification

Self justification became your ally as you struggled to maintain a world of fantasy where your self image went unchallenged. Where self pity was timid and reclusive, self justification was much bolder and provided emotional backup when negative feelings of guilt needed bolstering. Left to the imagination of self justification nothing was your fault as you only acted in defense of the injustice done to you by others.

*To know thyself must mean to know the malignancy of one's
Own instincts and to know as well one's power to deflect it.
Dr. Karl Menninger*

Mandalas
Seven & Eight

Conflicting
Self Image
(Good Child vs. Bad Child)

Your "Inner Child" is more complex than one believed to be insecure and helplessly subjective to outer forces. Mirroring the conflict within a ghost of your "good" childhood self image exists in direct opposition to a ghost of your "bad" childhood self image.

United only in the common purpose of survival, tearful tactics and false bravado underlies your childhood Primal Centering. Your "good" child cried softly and presented apology for transgressions. Your "bad" child often screamed in defiance and sought to get even for emotional injuries.

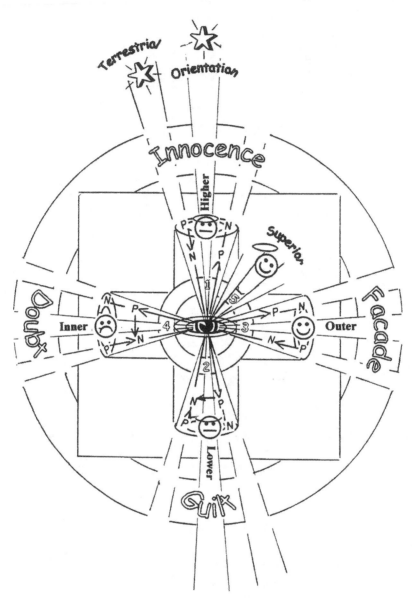

Superiority
Pseudo double positive self image

Shadows cast by the phantoms of self pity and self justification blocked from consciousness painful awareness of the insecurities and guilts of your Inner and Lower modes. A pseudo double positive idealized picture of self evolved of duplicity; simply misunderstood.

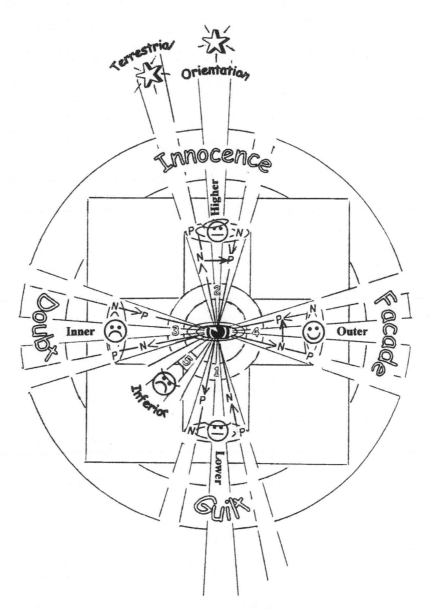

Inferiority
Pseudo double negative self image

Your Higher and Outer modes were often silenced giving free reign to self punishing thoughts claiming your central focus of emotion. This spirit of darkness came in the night, taunting you, reminding you that you were unworthy of love and acceptance. The repressed angry emotions of an unloved, unchosen child lie heavily in your subconscious mind and a centered emotional balance remained unattainable.

Mandala Nine

Claiming Your Emotional Ghosts

Every kingdom divided against

itself is brought to desolation.

Matthew 12.38

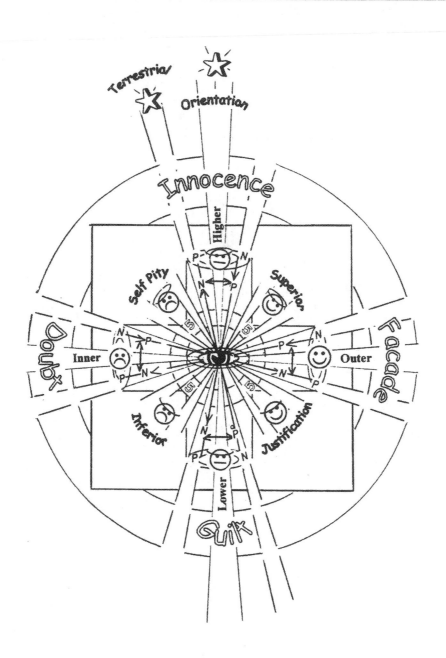

*The light in the eye of the beholder
Casts shadows on the world of reality*

Claiming Your Emotional Ghosts

The lighting of insight reveals the ghosts of childhood past as the transparent phantoms they are. Releasing these emotional ghosts to the light of your conscious mind sets in motion a journey into self understanding that is irreversible. Until this is done, the haunting memories of childhood will stay in the darkness of your subconscious mind causing you to forever look back over your shoulder for the causes of present day unhappiness. For those injuries done to you by your parents, for the jeers and rejections of your peers, for fate that placed you in defeating circumstances.

To realize your perceptions were that of a child is to realize, although the hurts were real, the plan behind your personal experience was to lead you to the moment when you are ready to accept full responsibility for your own life's experience. To accept responsibility for the person you have become is to claim power over the past and to view each unbidden memory to be relieved of its power to hurt you and instead become guides toward self realization.

The messages revealed by the lighting of your spiritual Center are sometimes harsh and sometimes beautiful, just as is life. If it hurts to look inside and find those things you would prefer to deny, it is also to find these things are illusions cast upon self and reality.

Viewing these Primal emotions from a wakeful center of insight reveals them not to be condemned but to be embraced in complete wakefulness as an evolutionary stage of emotional development. For every life there is a plan. Contained in the experiences of your childhood is the ultimate goal of enlightenment, for the questions you ask today rose from the confusions of yesterday.

Your evolutionary urges are wakened by your agreement to go forward in understanding of your Primal centering and by your refusal to stagnate in the belief systems which support the existence of a false sense of self. You will succeed in liberating yourself from the pull of Primal emotions when you place your trust in the divine plan for your personal evolution. Looking to the present for answers to your personal questions you release these questions to an intelligent universe. In doing so, you release the past and open to the spiritual guidance and balance that is your birthright.

You begin your rise from the ashes of your Primal centering the instant you take ownership and responsibility for bringing change. As you begin your freeing up process do not judge your negative emotions, merely watch them pass through you as transients. To feel guilt or self deprecation is to grant them validity and so to perpetuate them.

It is easy to see these Primal emotional responses being acted out by others. It is much more difficult to become aware of them existing in yourself. How quickly you grasp these revelations, as they apply to you, is an indication of your personal evolutionary emotional experience. If you see these faces, as they apply to others, and you surely do, you are equipped to begin the task of revealing them as existing within yourself. Your purpose is not to reflect yourself in the best possible light as you concentrate on the failings of others, but to free yourself from the belief that you are in need of such self deception.

* * * *

Willingness to recognize the malignancy of your ego defensive emotions, as learned in childhood, brightens the light of insight showing you the way. Your Primal self defensive emotions are instinctive and serve to provide the fundamental assurance of emotional survival. To the soul bent on spiritual evolvement these instinctive emotions must be at once accepted and rejected. Accepted in that they have served for a time and rejected in the name of further enlightenment and evolution.

* * * *

Your Dreaming Primal Consciousness

Dreaming of a perfect world where every one is equal and where love is the law, you have come to know the seeds of evolution inherent in your soul. In these experiences, it seems that self defense is no longer needed in a world of loving, caring souls. For a moment in time, the oneness of creation opens itself to you and serenity floods your being. You are startled from your reverie when adverse conditions threaten and you quickly arm yourself with Primal self defenses while yearning for yourdream to become your reality. A reality that seems destined to never be. Your Primal dreams are not often those of evolutionary growth for you feel you must direct your energies to the caring of your physical needs in order to survive in a material world. You dream, in Primal consciousness, of satisfying those needs through the acquisition of material wealth, as this appears to be the reigning God of this realm of existence, and you sorrow and justify your actions in attempt to bring balance in an unjust world and you sleep, believing you are awake . . .

Part Three

Reflections

of a

False Self Image

How Godlike, how immortal is he? But the slave and prisoner of his own opinion of himself. A fame won by his own deeds. Public opinion is a weak tyrant compared with our own private opinion. What a person thinks of himself, that is what determines, or rather indicates, his fate.

Henry David Thoreau

Mandala Ten

Know Thyself

There can be no intelligence comparable to the intelligence of self knowledge for all things you do are influenced by the self image you carry within you. Blindness to your own psychological makeup causes you to mistake emotional illusion for reality of self.

Your mental and physical strength is sapped through the energy it takes to support belief in a false self image. This illusionary self lives an imaginary self defeating existence. It is time to gather the forces of your mind and draw to the true Center of self awareness,.

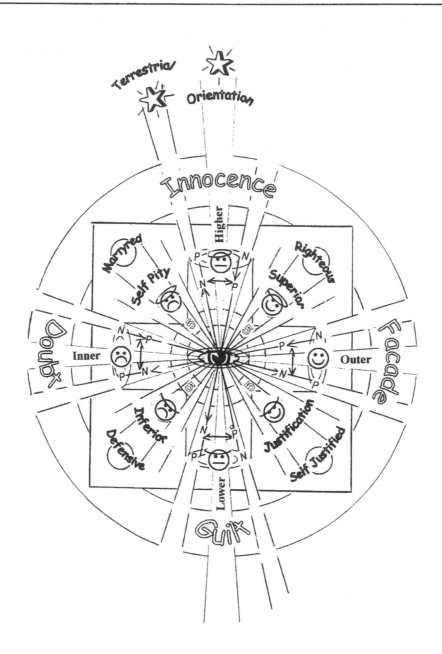

Primal Self Image

Righteous, defensive, blameless and martyred your Primal centering resulted in a grandiose sense of self seeded in illusion. Hidden from conscious view, buried deep in your subconscious mind, are self held beliefs you would never consciously recognize.

The Saint and the Sinner
are One in Primal consciousness

**I find a law then, that when I would do good,
evil is present with me... Romans 7.21 KJV**

The ghosts of your childhood self image undergo a personal transcendence in your eyes, becoming not merely innocent but martyred in the battle against the odds The Self Pitying ways of childhood are buried deep inside the martyr who does for others while resenting it. Vindicated, defensive and righteous, this template of disturbing emotions evolved of automatic reactions influencing your adult emotional experience. Existing in a state of complete emotional vulnerability, this false self image is constantly on the alert for attack. Righteous anger flares in defense of this illusionary self evolved of immature discernment.

You will not easily accept these immature emotional traits as existing in your adult self though you have relied on them for ego protection all of your life. You may feel as if your very existence is being threatened by this much self honesty but know this: A lighting of your spiritual center promises to lead you out of the darkness of self deception into the light of the whole person you are.

The beast born of illusion

As unknown, and yet well known;
As dying, and behold, we live;
As chastened and not killed.
Corinthians 6.9 KJV

In order to rid yourself of this beast that lives within, you must first recognize that he is there, to one degree or another,* in each and every one of us. The beast evolved of beliefs that he must be perfect, successful, and above all reproach. The beast is the imagined perfect self. He simply does not exist except in the imagination.

He is shocked at the outrageous conduct of others in which they appear to be selfish, grasping and cruel. He is self justification that blinds self to the reality that all people are basically the same, containing all those things that he contains. He is the beast born of rejection of self and others as imperfect human beings.

He is hate, he is revenge, he is judgment. He grew rigid and demanding of the material world as self evaluation unfolded and found itself lacking. The name of the beast is **fear**, fear for survival. He is not survival, instead he is self destruction pure and simple, as he pours forth bitterness, hate and violence against self and the world.

* There are as many states of emotional evolvement as there are people. You may experience few or many of the emotions common to the Primal consciousness. Self honesty, however, is mandatory in your successful journey to Centered Grace.

Do not sleep as do others...

Unrecognized and so free to continue jerking your emotions first this way and that, you are at the mercy of your own creation. This false sense of self has become your nemesis; your God or Goddess of retribution. This false self image fights for survival and this fight is its undoing for as the faces of righteousness, defensive anger, martyrdom and self justification show themselves to you they lose the power to hold you captive.

Many times you will be drawn into the negative currents of your Primal consciousness for these ways have been with you for a lifetime. Allow these emotionally painfully experiences to prompt insights, revealing and healing the falseness that steals away your peace and happiness. Know that when you lose control of yourself during adverse conditions, you become a living breathing demonstration of negativity, you become the anger and the hate of the world. Know that when you experience true love and compassion for a fellow human being you radiate love, you radiate compassion. To know that "I am the love of the world" and "I am the hate of the world" is a revelation. To believe you experience love or hate as transient emotions apart from who you are is a far different thing than to know, in the moment, **you bring to life** that thing you express.

Compassionate Self Observation

When at times, you become angry and defensive, do not view these feelings as thieves stealing your peace of mind for serenity also comes of recognizing these feelings with quiet observation. As you view your negative feelings with compassionate self awareness, a part of yourself has evolved into a state of objective awareness. With this insightful observation, minus emotional condemnation, comes release as you experience less and less of that which no longer flourishes in darkness.

Insight comes in brief flashes of understanding. As these lightings fade into memory, you may slip back into slumber as darkness falls before your eyes. Even as this happens, your experience has brought change with the promise of who you can be as the lightings eventually dissipate the ways of your Primal nature for lack of confirmation.

You may wonder at your new found peaceful viewing of the world around you as you come to understand yourself. You may wonder, that at times as you experience the negative emotions of your Primal centering, with clear understanding of their misconceived origins, you no longer believe in their truths.

Part Four

Celestial Horizons

One can never repeat too often that reason as it exists in humanity, is only your intellectual eye, and that for the eye to see, it needs the light of heaven.
Anon.

Emotional Evolution

Each stage of a lifetime is an incarnation of the last in a constant evolution of the life experience. The baby disappears from view and in his place the youth of ten assumes bravado which is given over to the one of twenty who no longer questions because he already knows.

Yet another incarnation begins as the fires begin to cool and questioning begins anew. Each stage of a lifetime appears as a different incarnation occupying one changeable form. During these incarnations, somehow life loses its luster and defeat becomes hard to bear. As each incarnation beckons with the promise of peace, the one who demands less of life and more of self is born replacing the youth who's dreams have died.

One soul is the common thread connecting these evolutionary lifetimes as one disappears, yet remains, as each image dies, yet lives, becoming another. This micro-structure reflects a macro experience of a lifetime, living the many incarnations of the spirit of life in search of enlightenment

Mandala Eleven

Lighting the Halo
of a Heavenly Body

And as we have born the image of the earthly

We shall also bear the image of the heavenly.

Corinthians 15.49 KJV

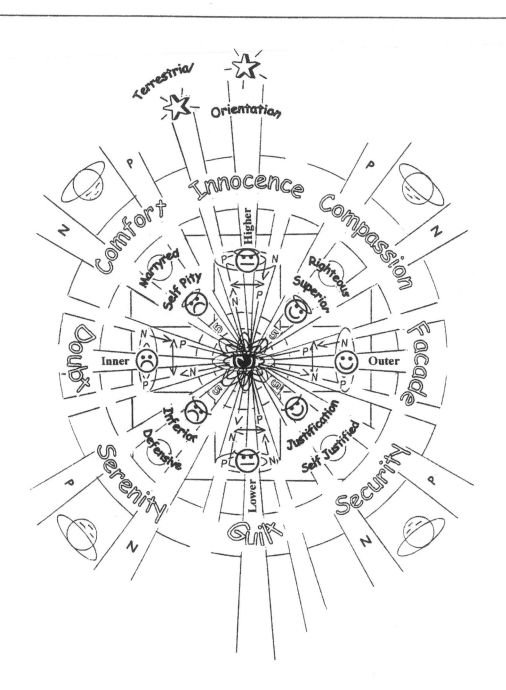

Four Spirits of Completion

That their hearts might be comforted, being knit together in love. And to all the riches of the full assurance of understanding, to the acknowledgement of the mystery of God.

Four Spirits of Completion:

Comfort -Security- Compassion - Serenity

Through healing rays of light you wake from the darkness of your Primal Centering. The negative energies of your false self image are released to the lighting of insight. Unlike your Primal modes which rely on opposing forces to maintain their energies, your Spiritual modes exist in harmonious support of one another. These four spirits, that are one, work in tandem for the common cause of opening your spiritual eye so you may see through and beyond the darkness of your Primal centering. These four Spirits of emotional evolution are not strangers to you for you have known of them all your life:

*Your **Comfort** may have gone unnoticed by your inability to overcome the challenges life has put before you.*

*Your sense of **Security** may have been denied by your need to amass material things in hopes of proving self worth.*

*Your experience of **Compassion** and altruistic love may have been blocked by the conditional love you imposed on both yourself and others.*

*Your **Serenity** may have been stolen by your fears of unworthiness and a need to defend.*

As you meld in consciousness with your Four Spirits of Completion you view the ways of your false sense of self with insight for the only thing blocking your experience of your spiritual modes of completion is your belief in falseness:

As you release self pitying , self defeating
ways:
Comfort happens!

As you release self doubt and self justification:
Security happens!

As you release conditional love and judgment:
Compassion happens!

As you release feelings of inferiority and
defensive anger:
Serenity happens!

It is not for you to **create** these modes of completion, it is only for you to accept that they are integral part of who you already are! You only need to keep a watchful Centered eye on negative thoughts and emotions springing from the past. If your memories are tainted with blame and accusations and all the angry helpless feelings that accompany these thoughts, let them be revealed to you now in the lighting of your spiritual insight thereby **allowing** your emotional evolution to happen.

The Spirit of Comfort

The Spirit of Comfort reveals the uselessness of self pity, exposing these feelings as thieves stealing your true strengths. Vow to never again project your precious energies into these waves of weakness, eventually culminating in the helplessness you placed your belief in.

The Spirit of Security

Consider the need to justify your actions to yourself or to others as indications of a self doubting and insecure Primal self image asserting itself. When you lay this burden down you will be filled with a sense of wonder as the hard shell of protection, you thought you needed, falls away. Freedom from thoughts of a self justifying nature will be tested sorely, as you have lived with this Primal instinct for a lifetime. Any reference, real or imagined that tends to endanger your sense of self worth activates old familiar emotional patterns. You must remember, you live in a world of angels in transition, some of these are held captive by their own insecurities. Because of this they too labor under the illusion that they must be perfect in order to be loved. Become acutely aware of the differences in people and allow these differences to be, both in self and others, for your truth shall set you free and this is your goal.

Become as a Child

Let not your heart be troubled, neither let it be afraid
Matthew 14.KJV

To be afraid is to be poised against assault that may or may not come. **It is the fear that is the assault.** So it is, in the absence of fear, the bliss of Spiritually Centered comfort and security become personal experience. Your Centered experience of comfort and security is that of your unwavering faith and belief in your ability to face and conquer life's challenges. The will to survive, clearly blessed in a state of grace and peace, signals your conscious awareness of your guiding spirit within.

Healing of emotional (or physical) pain must first become a healing of the mind where spirit and matter come together in consciousness, functioning as **one**. To doubt this unity is to short circuit the power of your faith. To experience the comfort and security of your spiritual Centering, as an integral part of your very essence is to convert the negative energies of doubt into positive healing light energies radiating through out your entire being.

Serenity

The evening star shines from a heart emptied of bitterness for things not understood. You observe the atrocities occurring on earth and you try to understand, but you do not, and you think "Some day I will understand God's plan and the reason why these things exist". And you turn away pretending to yourself that is answer enough. You bury your despair and you seek the serenity of mind God has promised you and it does not come. And in your heart you ask, "What kind of God allows these things to be"? Rage, held secret in your heart fuels your anger at those challenges of faith God has put before you. You will not be struck down at these admissions for your God already knows what is in your heart. When you are ready, you will sense the angels smile as you release these buried feelings out into the healing light.

The darkness that appears to cast out the lighting of earth at times, is the darkness of the human spirit asleep to its truth. If you would change the world think on these things:

Whatsoever things are true, whatsoever things are honest,
whatsoever things are just, whatsoever things are lovely,
whatsoever things are of good report, if there be any virtue
and if there be any praise think on these things.

Philippians 4.8 KJV

Compassion

Finally, be you all of one mind,
Having compassion one of another.
John 2.19 KJV

First, be of one mind in yourself, be of your Spiritual Centering. True compassion for your own confusions opens your insight into the nature of others. Ask that this perfect love fill you with human understanding.

Your Primal Centering evolved of fears of unworthiness. Your Spiritual Centering is founded in the acceptance of the nonjudgmental love of your creator. Your Primal Centering has caused you to be afraid to love unconditionally, afraid your love will not be returned. If it is not, so be it, for you are grounded in self worth not subject to the confusions of others. Remember that just as life presents challenges for your own growth, so it is with others. When you view others, at times, walking in darkness, see them not as evil, but in search of the light just as you.

May you begin each morning with compassion for the human condition as a newness in understanding tempers your view of the world. Heavenly compassion is not merely sorrow for another less fortunate than your self. The pureness of this compassion feels another's pain with no reference to self at all. You watch others living out trials you have been spared and you know these sacrifices are in part for your own salvation, for we are all **one**.

Mandala Twelve

Rebirth

(Your Star in Zenith)

There are stars terrestrial and stars celestial
But one star differs from another in glory.

Corinthians 15.40 KJV

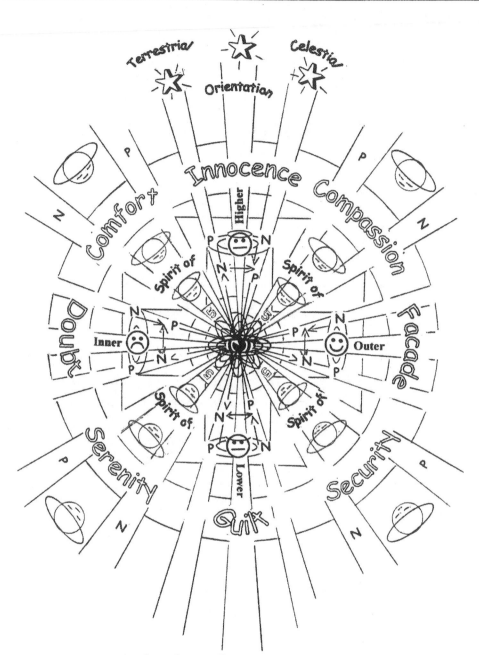

Star of Celestial Consciousness

There are also celestial bodies and bodies terrestrial,
But the glory of the celestial is one and the glory of
The terrestrial is another.
Corinthians 15.41 KJV

Your Star in Zenith

Rebirth

As the spiritual lighting of your primal consciousness comes to rest, a brilliant star reappears on the celestial horizon. This lighting is symbolic of your soul self, your higher self, your celestial twin, your destiny. One with the primal channel of innocence you often confused this innocence of self with spiritual evolvement. The lighting of your star in zenith exists beyond opposing forces and is not subject to the polaristic pull of your Primal centering.

You do not merely share your consciousness with this angelic spirit, you are an angel in physical form reawakening to the truth of who you are. As you wake to this awareness, holy lighting fills you from within. You are the Alpha and the Omega, both the beginning and the end, the lowest and the highest. In this all encompassing form the universe finds expression through your consciousness.

The raising of consciousness that is the wedding of spirit and matter is one of evolution for spirit and matter have existed as one since the beginning of time. As you come to realize the light within is the true light of your existence you return there for your truths and trust in the guidance. Recognizing your spirituality as an intelligent guide must not remain as merely a mental concept. This spirit of life is the truth of who you are. Your Celestial consciousness is your first state of living consciousness, your Center of creative energy, your eye of intuition into the mystery of life. It is through these insightful visions you are able to view the ways of your false sense of self removed from the sting of self recrimination. This is the you that refuses to say no to life's challenges and dares to tear the mask of illusion from your vision. It is here, in a meditative state, that you renew the wonder, as you release the falseness of self you believed to be you.

Mandala Thirteen

As Above - So Below

Star of Grace

For he is our peace who has made both one and has broken down the middle wall of partition between us that He might reconcile both into one body.

Ephesians 2.15 KJV

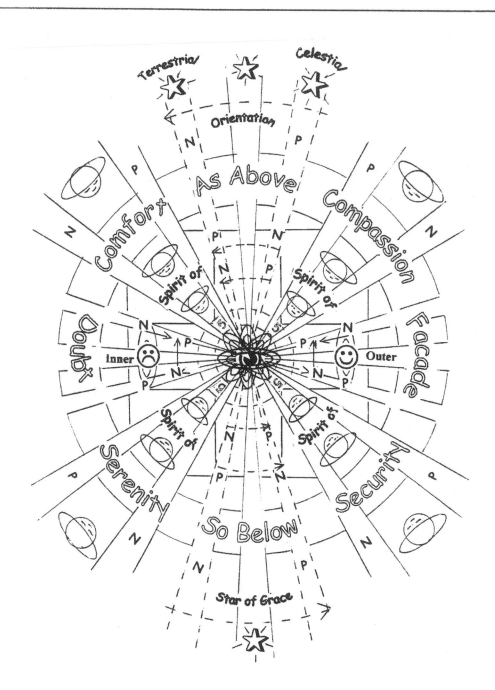

Star of Grace

As oscillating auras of light trace the path of a Harmonic celestial axis, joining your Terrestrial and Celestial consciousness as one, a star appears on the southern celestial horizon signaling your absolution.

For by Grace you are saved by faith
And not that of yourself, it is the gift of God.
Ephesians 2.8 KJV

As Above - So Below

With the star of earthly orientation overhead and the star of Grace at your feet, that which appeared to be Higher fuses with that which appeared to be Lower and at once you see the truth of your spiritually Centered existence; **your fall from Grace was an illusion cast upon reality,** just as good and evil itself is non-existent in universal truth founded in perpetual unity and harmony.

The Trinity of mind, body and spirit

In the joining of your Spiritual consciousness with your Primal consciousness, expanding the boundaries of your Primal Centering, new horizons beckon you to wake to the realization that the self same energies that sustain the ONENESS of the universe are one and the same with your life force. To be consciously aware of your spirituality as a stabilizing source of comfort and direction is to be re-born into a state of emotional balance. To be re-born is to experience the Grace that eluded you as you dwelt in Primal consciousness believing you were alone.

Become as a Child

In your re-born state of Spiritual consciousness look to your Higher Mode for edification and self forgiveness rather than self judgment. Allow the freedom of self acceptance to join in Centered agreement with your Lower Mode bringing the Grace of absolution. This is a Centering technique you must first apply to self before you will see clearly enough to place judgment on others. When you have come to recognize your own frailties through self forgiveness there will be little judgment of others.

* * * *

There is no such thing as being so "good", that you are released from the damning influence of the self inflicted tortures of guilt. There is no such thing as being so "bad" that you are not forgiven by the spirit within.

Happy is the one that condemneth not in self
That thing that is allowed.
Romans 14.22 KJV

* * * *

Mandala Fourteen

As Within So Without

The Morning Star of Emancipation

The Evening Star of Reconciliation

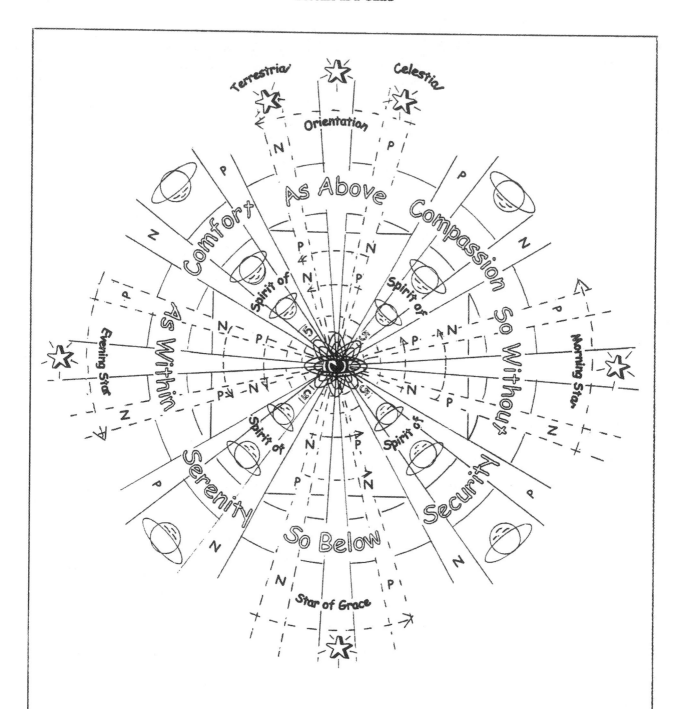

The stillness of Centered consciousness reveals the equality of all things restoring your emotional equilibrium. Flexibility replaces rigid Primal vision as the morning and evening stars cast the light of emancipation and reconciliation upon the landscape before you.

As Within - So Without

With the dawning of spiritual insight, the morning star of emancipation casts out the illusions of separation clouding your vision. The evening star of reconciliation completes an axis of emotional equilibrium lighting your horizon. As the oneness that you are is revealed as the living Center of your being, the circuitry of your inner vs. outer Primal Modes becomes still and quiet in total self acceptance.

In a Spiritual Centering of Primal polarities let there be no conscious effort to change those things about yourself you find unacceptable for that need will never be fulfilled by a judgmental mind. **Instead, let there be an experience of center cleansing of the need to change** as the Grace of absolution permeates your being restoring you to your legacy of wholeness; just as you are.

To Thine Own Self Be True

The great paradox of the message of the Mandalas of Centered light is while your Primal Centering exposes you to a painful viewing of yourself, you are assured this condition is not to be condemned, but understood in the quest for enlightenment. Your spiritual evolution is not a matter of attempting to become a better person either in your own eyes or the eyes of others. Enlightenment is about feeling good in your skin, independent of conditions. In this way your evolvement is experienced only by the amount of peace and joy you feel and give to life.

You have only to accept yourself as worthy to obtain release from the evaluations of society. You have only to accept yourself in your shared condition of the imperfect human race to experience a harmonious Centering of your self image. Forgiveness and acceptance of a much higher nature lives within your heart and by releasing false beliefs you carry regarding your self worth you will come to know it and to live from it as a source of internal orientation not dependent on the proving of self, but of simple acceptance of self requiring no proof. Your goal is a releasing of pretense and a need to appear to be other than you are, to be true to yourself regardless of exterior influences and opinions.

Decide to release yourself from the pain of the self judgment that must be endured by those who honor differences as determiners of worth. Wait patiently for the lighting of your insight when you will see all your differences as God given expressions of life to be exalted   in the simplicity of **being** with nothing to pretend and nothing to defend.

The Centering of Your Inner/Outer Modes

The degree of Centering you have and will achieve is revealed to you in your self reflections as you inter-act with others and society in general. Your goal is a releasing of the need to appear other than you are and to release the insecurities this need promotes. To be true to yourself , in spite of exterior influences is the key to freedom and true Spiritual Centering.

The material world is malleable, plaint, and giving, when seeing from the flexibility of your Centered self. As you grow in knowledge of your oneness with the universe you no longer view others as threats to your identity and security. No one other than yourself holds the keys to your success in life. When others do not accept your ways as theirs it is because they are not. Leave these people to walk their paths in peace and you in yours. Your paths crossed for a purpose and if you experience personal conflict allow their behaviors to remind you of a likeness in yourself you no longer choose to experience.

* * * *

Portrait of Your Centered Self

"Through my beliefs, I became me, a unique spark of the Universal consciousness. I stand Centered and grounded between the sea of opposites and have chosen 'this over that' as guide lines for my existence. These guide lines serve to aid me in my search for individualism. I see these beliefs as something apart from my Centered self, and do not give them the power to stifle my growth as a person, for it is only when I mistake these beliefs for myself that I become outraged if anyone threatens to undermine these beliefs. In my state of self- approval, I leave you to your peace. In your state of self - approval, you leave me to mine. In this state of mutual agreement we can work together for the betterment of humanity".

* * * *

Part Five

Harmonic Centering

Constant in their celestial design of light and configuration, the heavenly galaxy of stars and planets, have from the beginning of time, charmed the souls of earthly inhabitants. It seems the mystery of life is revealed as you gaze toward the heavens and sense your unity with the Universe. And you know there surely is a heaven, because of the holiness you feel at this communion. And you know heaven to be an integral part of who you are for as you see it, so it is.

Mandala Fifteen

Star Of

Universal Harmonics

All that is visible must go beyond itself,
Extend into the realm of the invisible.
Thereby it receives its true consecration and clarity
And takes firm root in the cosmic order.

The Cauldron, I Ching

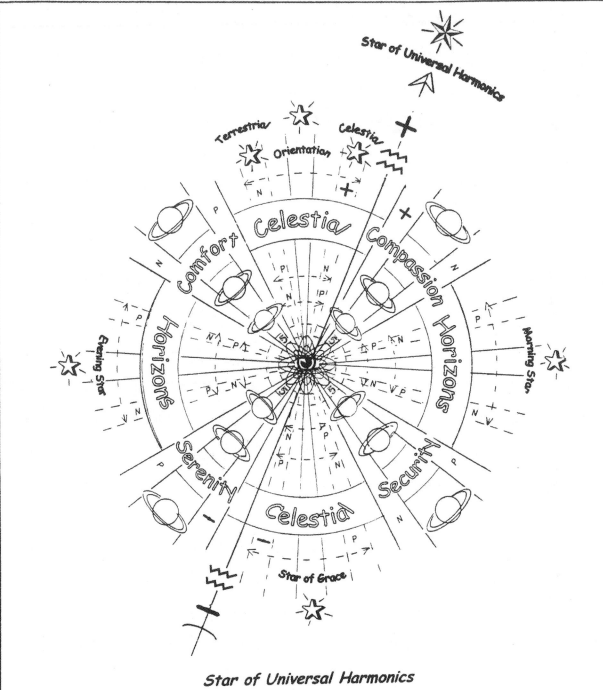

Star of Universal Harmonics
(Axis of Center Grounding)

Mimicking the light and darkness of creation itself
your Center of Wholeness joins opposing emotional
forces as **One** in Harmony and Unity.

Rooted and Grounded in Love

Eph 111.17

The Seventh Star of Universal Harmonics, cast outwardly as a symbol of your Harmonic Centering lights the North star above you and the Southern star of Grace at your feet. Even as the morning and evening stars of the East and West light the familiar horizon you took for reality the great circle of the celestial sphere called the true horizon reveals the boundlessness of your expanded universal consciousness.

The wedding of Spirit and Matter

The energies of the Center of Universal Harmonics represent a union of spirit and matter oscillating at the speed of light beyond measurement. In a slowing down of this oscillation matter appears in solid observable form. Although the life generated by this union appears in infinitesimal forms, the self same source exists as the center of all creation. Acceptance and acknowledgment of your spiritual existence (anti-matter) and your physical being (matter) opens the doors of creation to your vision.

Your brain acts as a receptor and distributor of this perfect energy. As an outlet for this creative energy, your brain fires neurons connecting you with the **one** from which it came and from which it is. Your perception of life as an individual demonstration of this Universal perfect energy determines the paths this energy will ultimately travel. As you release false beliefs of who you are, healing energies are freed to follow their natural course throughout your mind, body, and life experience. Fear, worry, and anxiety all stem from the mental image of a false sense of self you have created. Release this imaginary image and you release the universal harmonic energy to the freedom of creating your experience of the living, loving, graces of your God.

Visualization

Imagine the Universe as light energy held in form by an inner knowledge of itself. Imagine the earth's surface beneath your feet as moving molecules of this energy, attracting and repelling but always knowing what it is; a configuration of a planet suspended in space by the idea of itself. Imagine other planets and all the stars in the heavens to be observable forms of this self same intelligence

Imagine your own body to be an idea of a perfect manifestation. of this light energy in material form. As you stand on the earth's surface, as a self held idea of form,
become aware of your physical contact with the earth's surface as bodies exchanging ideas. Feel your own energy becoming the earth's energy, feel the earth's energy becoming your energy. The gravitational inter-change is one of buoyant healing energy

as you release tension in the knowledge that you are the stuff of the earth and stars released to the freedom of personal physical action.

.   Mentally move yourself outwardly through this vision. Feel yourself flowing freely, intermingling with the world of structure, become aware of your body as unrestricted form. Sense the currents of air flowing around you, as you walk about, displacing space with your physicalness.

Become aware that you are no different from the space you displace. You are not separate, you are simply serving to bring form to that which is ethereal, that which permeates the universe. When as a child, you ran barefoot in the rain, raising your face to drink of the water as it fell upon you... you were unaware of where your child-self ceased to be and the rain began.

Heartbeat of the universe

The rhythm in walking, The rhythm in talking,
The horses gait, The flow of the tides,
The hum of a motor, The tick of a clock,
The clapping of hands, The dancing feet.
The rhythmic beat of LIFE.

Mandala Sixteen

Quintessence

Allow your emotions to resonate with the music of the angels for it is not self imperfection that is discordant. It is in self rejection that harsh vibrations interrupt the lyrical scales of celestial harmony.

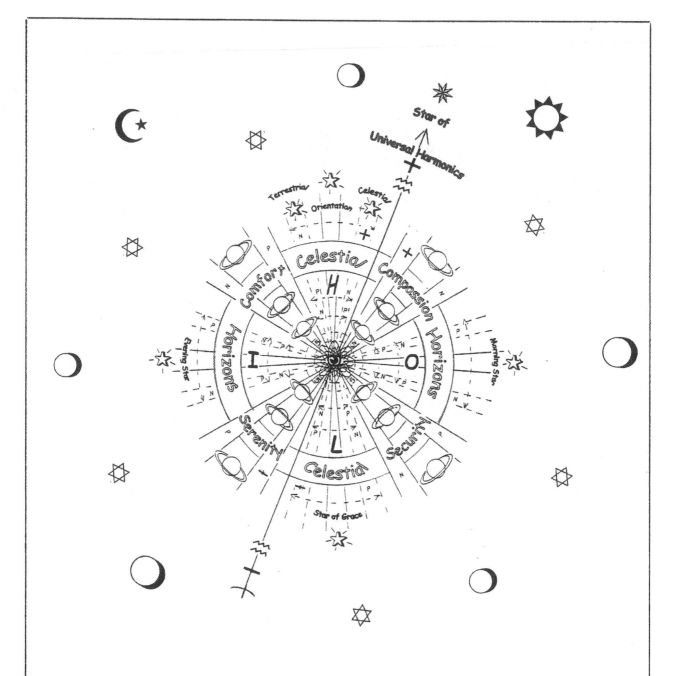

No need to wonder why I'm here
No role must I rehearse
For I find in God's great plan
I am the Universe

M.G. LaBounty

Quintessence

The ultimate centering of your emotional consciousness is rooted in the circuitry of your Primal centering so that what appeared to perpetuate duality and emotional imbalance, reveals a Spiritual evolution grounded in universal truths of harmony and unity.

The <u>H</u>igher, <u>O</u>uter, <u>L</u>ower, <u>I</u>nner, modes of Primal consciousness become One in the HOLI-ness of a mind grounded in complete and total self acceptance.

Walk as children of the light

As a young child you saw from your spiritual center and the openness and acceptance of that which you saw carried with it not one tiny grain of judgement. Each new discovery simply was - wonderful and exciting. You remember how you grew to lose the wonder as your eyes lost their luster and the world became dull and gray, lost in the blankness of by gone yesterdays and the tomorrows that never came. You lost communion with your guiding angel who waited for the sunrise of your second birthing when you would walk again in consciousness as a child of the light.

*"... and the end of all our exploring will be
to arrive where we started and to know
the place for the first time".*

The dullness of the material world you viewed in Primal consciousness is glorified with the light of spirit now visible to your vision; not changing form but redefining the nature of what you see. You know you have been here before, yet each thing is transformed, appearing translucent and ethereal, solid and yet transparent, as if the hard edges of material definition were removed.

You feel as renewed as the visions appearing before you, and you know you are in a place of oneness where all things combine in a climactic explosion of completion. You see that in the joining, the impact, the explosion, you came to life in visible form. You see that your visible form appeared of the anti-matter of nothingness and that which would be invisible spirit became visible in body.

With the reconciliation of these fundamental opposites, the doors of all creation open before your eyes. Recognition of your spiritual/physical existence as one brings the bliss of unified self awareness. The wholeness that you are at this union is the eye of your God consciousness where all things come together in an order so perfect you stand in awe of the world revealed to you as it is appears glorified with the light of spirit. Just as you are inspired by the beauty of the sunset all things are transformed by the beauty of acceptance before your eyes.

You are all the children of the light;
And the children of the day,
You are not of the night or darkness.
Theolossians 5.5 KJV.

<u>Epilogue</u>

NOW

If all of your yesterdays were gathered into bouquets

Of memories

And all of your tomorrows, shining with untold glory,

Were to fill all of space eternal, they could not

Together

Hold the fragrance or add the light of one small candle

To the only time you will ever really know;

The moment that is NOW!

As you emerge from the cocoon of a false sense of self you find you are the creator of the instant that is now and that only in this instant does creation exist. The structure of yesterday and tomorrow fades from your consciousness as you wake to the infinite glory that is contained in the moment. It is in the quiet between thoughts of the past and the worries of tomorrow that the glory of life reveals itself. These quiet times, become those times of blissful awareness of being alive in the simple pleasures of your day, the yearned for fulfillment, the consummate experience. Perfect, profound, complete, filling a deficiency, a wanting deep inside that cannot be filled by exterior means.

Be not conformed to this world,

Be transformed by the renewing of your mind.

Romans 12.2

Your search for insight into your true self must be an integral part of your daily life and not be considered a separate thing to be contemplated, discussed and left behind. For an expedient integration to occur you must live your life each day, from two different levels of awareness, that which looks out and that which looks in.

If you feel at times as if the spiritual lighting has gone out and you suffer the emotional pain of aloneness, know that it is you who have turned away and know that even in those moments of darkness what you are experiencing contains the potential for enlightenment. Look for the lesson you must learn, even as you are hurting, and do not condemn these feelings. When you are able to do this, you are joining in consciousness with the Centered Light that is guiding you out of darkness.

What has been and what will be only appears to exist. At the Center of your heart, in the moment, lies the answers to your questions. Indeed, in this centering you will find there are no questions, only a sense of completion, a coming together of spirit and matter. As a living being you bring this instant into visual perspective and even though your focus is at times lost in the past or projected into an imaginary future, the Center lighting does not go out, cannot go out for it is the eternal light of creation itself. As your spiritual eye is opened many things will be revealed to you bringing you ever closer to the ultimate state of Grace that lives within you.

There is much in the nature of humanity that will undergo a transformation as the evolution between spirit and matter unfolds. This transformation will not come of shame and guilt as sins committed against the laws of heaven, for heaven does not recognize sin. With each challenge met and conquered, you begin to return to the earth the realizations of the heavens.

Whatever you shall bind on earth,
Shall be bound in heaven:
And what so ever you shall loose on earth
Shall be loosed in heaven.
Matthew 18.18 KJV

There are many who consciously walk the Celestial/Terrestrial path at this time. Each day many more come to the realization as to why they are here and what their true purpose is. As the masses awake to this understanding heaven and earth will be joined, in consciousness, and the differences in humanity will be apparent only in physical forms and not in the mind sets of these celestial/terrestrial beings, one to the other, each and the same.

Grace Be Unto Thee